Why *Voting* Matters

Who Can Vote?

Kristen Rajczak Nelson

PowerKiDS press.
NEW YORK

Published in 2019 by The Rosen Publishing Group, Inc.
29 East 21st Street, New York, NY 10010

Editor: Elizabeth Krajnik
Book Design: Rachel Rising

Photo Credits: Cover Hill Street Studios/Blend Images/Getty Images; Cover (background), pp. 1, 3, 4 ,6, 8, 10, 12, 14, 16, 18, 20, 22, 23, 24 PepinoVerde/Shutterstock.com; p. 5 Lisa F. Young/Shutterstock.com; p. 7 Everett Historical/Shutterstock.com; p. 9 Burlingham/Shutterstock.com; p. 11 Keith Bell/Shutterstock.com; p.13 Megan Betteridge/Shutterstock.com; p. 15 (top) Tom Williams/ CQ-Roll Call Group/Getty Images; p. 15 (bottom) Bill Clark/CQ-Roll Call Group/Getty Images; p. 17 RHONA WISE/AFP/Getty Images; p. 19 sirtravelalot/Shutterstock.com; p. 21 Hero Images/Getty Images; p. 22 chekart/Shutterstock.com.

Cataloging-in-Publication Data

Names: Rajczak Nelson, Kristen.
Title: Who can vote? / Kristen Rajczak Nelson.
Description: New York : PowerKids Press, 2019. | Series: Why voting matters | Includes index.
Identifiers: LCCN ISBN 9781538330173 (pbk.) | ISBN 9781538330159 (library bound) | ISBN 9781538330180 (6 pack)
Subjects: LCSH: Voting--United States--Juvenile literature. | Elections--United States--Juvenile literature. | Political participation--United States--Juvenile literature.
Classification: LCC JK1978.R35 2019 | DDC 324.60973--dc23

Manufactured in the United States of America

CPSIA Compliance Information: Batch #CS18PK For further information contact Rosen Publishing, New York, New York at 1-800-237-9932.

Contents

The Right to Vote

U.S. **citizens** choose their own leaders by voting. They vote for local leaders, such as mayors. They also vote for national leaders, including the president and members of Congress. The right to vote is one of the basic rights listed in the U.S. Constitution. This is the highest law of the country.

STATION #3
STATION #4
VOLUNTEER

Votes for All

When the United States was founded in 1776, only some white men had the right to vote. The 15th Amendment, or change, to the Constitution gave black men the right to vote. For many years, women fought for this right. Then, in 1920, the 19th Amendment gave women the right to vote, too.

WOMAN SUFFRAGE
HEADQUARTERS.
MEN OF OHIO!
GIVE THE WOMEN A SQUARE DEAL
Vote For Amendment Nº 23 On September 3-1912.
COME IN AND LEARN
WHY WOMEN
OUGHT to Vote.

Hometown Voter

To vote in a U.S. **election** today, a person must be a U.S. citizen. Citizens are people who live in a country and have the rights that country's laws give them. Voters must be 18 years old on or before the next Election Day. They also must live in their state for a certain amount of time.

You Have to Sign Up!

Citizens have to register, or sign up, in their state in order to vote. When they register, many people choose to join a **political party**. Sometimes, states have laws about when voters need to register. Missing this deadline, or final day, might mean a person can't vote in an election!

Voter Registration Application
review the General, Application, and State
This space for office
the United States of America?
old on or before election day?
in response to either of these questions, do not complete form.
instructions for rules regarding eligibility to register prior to age 18.)
First Name
Middle
Last Name
Apt. or Lot #
City/Town
Where You Get Your Mail If Different From Above
Telephone Number (optional)
5
6
ID
Month
Day
Year
8
Race or Ethnic Group
(see item 8 in the instructions for your State)
of Party
7 in the instructions foy your State)
instructions and I swear/affirm that:

Voting Away from Home

U.S. citizens who live in another state or country or serve in the armed forces can also vote. These voters have to sign up through their state to receive a special voting form called an **absentee ballot**. They mark their choice and mail in this form to cast their vote.

U.S. ARMY

In U.S. Territories

People who live in the U.S. **territories** of Guam, the U.S. Virgin Islands, the Northern Mariana Islands, and Puerto Rico are U.S. citizens. People living in American Samoa are U.S. **nationals**. Those who register in these places can vote in many U.S. elections, such as elections for members of Congress.

Puerto Rico
con
ROMNEY
RYAN

GUAM

But Not for President

However, people who live in U.S. territories can't vote for president. In presidential elections, a group of people who represent, or act in place of, registered voters in their state cast votes. This is called the Electoral College. U.S. territories aren't included in the Electoral College.

CAMPAIGN 2016
2016 Electoral College Map

In Jail

People who carry out certain crimes often can't vote while in **jail**. After they get out of jail, some states make them wait for a set amount of time before they can vote again. A few states make them apply to get back their voting rights. In some states, they can't vote again at all.

COUNTY
JAIL

Those of All Abilities Can Vote

People with **disabilities** also have the right to vote. They may have a hard time getting to a polling place or understanding the activity. But, they can have a friend, family member, or caregiver help them. Sometimes these people are told they aren't allowed to vote. However, only a judge can rule someone unable to vote.

VOTE
HERE
I VOTED
VOTE

Voters' Voices

Today, almost all American citizens can register to vote. No matter what a person's race or religious beliefs are or how much money they have, they can vote. Voting gives citizens a voice in government. It helps leaders know what citizens think and want!

Glossary

absentee ballot: A vote cast by mail before an election by a voter who isn't able to vote in person at the time of the election.

citizen: A person who lives in a country and has the rights given to them by that country's laws.

disability: A condition, such as an illness or injury, that limits or changes how someone moves or thinks.

election: The act of gathering to cast votes to choose someone as a leader.

jail: A place where people who have carried out a crime must stay.

national: A person who is from a country or a country's territory but may not be a citizen of that country.

political party: A group of people that has the same ideas about how the government should be run.

territory: One of the parts of the United States that is not a state.

Index

Websites

Due to the changing nature of Internet links, PowerKids Press has developed an online list of websites related to the subject of this book. This site is updated regularly. Please use this link to access the list: www.powerkidslinks.com/wvm/wcv

Words to Know

goal

piano

skate

soccer

Work hard every day!